Crossway

A play

Jane Parry-Davies

Samuel French – London
New York – Sydney – Toronto – Hollywood

CROSSWAYS

First produced in March, 1987, for the Cornish Federation of Women's Institutes' Drama Festival by Stoke Climsland Women's Institute with the following cast of characters:

Mrs Rowe	Shirley Burton
Elizabeth/Sarah	Kathryn Clark
1st Caller	Jenny Llewellyn
2nd Caller	Sue Wiltshire
Caroline	Diane Wilsteed
Dr Margery Johnston	Kathy Haines
Mrs Duncan	Vere Fisher

Produced by Jane Parry-Davies

Crossways was awarded first prize for the best original script, with Kathryn Clark receiving the award for best actress for her performance as Elizabeth/Sarah.

CHARACTERS

Mrs Rowe: brisk, capable, middle-class, middle-aged

Elizabeth: her daughter, widowed two years previously and gradually resuming her life

1st Caller
2nd Caller } females researching ancient buildings in the parish

Caroline: a close friend of Elizabeth, amusing, scatty but very likeable

Dr Margery Johnston: psychiatrist with an enquiring turn of mind

Mrs Duncan: the rector's wife

The action takes place in the sitting-room of an ancient cottage

CROSSWAYS

The sitting-room of an ancient cottage into which Elizabeth has just moved

There is a door UL opening into the hall. The wall R is dominated by an open fireplace in which a log fire is burning with a set of fire-irons on the hearth and a large rug in front. There is a couch facing front, a coffee table, a pouffe and two armchairs. DL is a small desk and chair with a telephone. Against the back wall is a table, or small dresser, with two bottles of wine and a tray holding wine glasses. (Please see the ground plan on page 20.) There is a "window" in the fourth "wall"

As the CURTAIN *rises, Elizabeth is finishing a flower arrangement on the* US *table and Mrs Rowe, her mother, is placing a final ornament on the mantelpiece*

Mrs Rowe (*standing back and looking round the room*) There, that's the lot. You really are lucky, Elizabeth. Not a single thing lost or broken. Removal firms must be better nowadays than when we moved down here.

Elizabeth (*looking towards her mother*) Yes, they were good. I should have hated losing anything. (*Putting the last flower in the bowl*) It was so difficult to decide what to bring when I was selling up. I still don't know if I made the right choice.

Mrs Rowe I think you did. This room looks very pretty; all the rooms do.

A shower of sparks flies out from the fire on to the rug. Mrs Rowe sweeps up

Oh dear, this rug will be ruined if you are not careful.

Elizabeth (*placing the bowl of flowers on the desk*) I have been
looking for a fire-guard, but they are all so modern, and the wrong
shape. I meant to use only the central heating, but a fire seemed right
in here, somehow, and it makes the room seem brighter. I'm not used
to the small windows yet.

Mrs Rowe And you'll miss the space you had at Moorfield, too. Why
you couldn't move in with Daddy and me after Peter was killed, I shall
never know.

Elizabeth (*turning to her mother in exasperation*) Oh, Mother, let's
not go over that again. I know I couldn't have gone on living at
Moorfield without Peter but I wanted my own things around me. It
was bad enough selling the house, and so much we had bought
together, like Peter dying all over again, and, oh, I don't know, like a
betrayal somehow.

Mrs Rowe You could have used our granny flat, and ... sorry, my dear,
I'm being an interfering mother again. Of course you must live your
own life; and Crossways is charming.

Elizabeth You know, it's like fate. I've been through this village
dozens of times, and if there hadn't been a diversion when the main
road was closed, I should never have found Crossways. I knew I'd live
here as soon as I saw it, thatched roof and all. I could picture every
room before I had even opened the gate. As if I had lived here before.

Mrs Rowe (*going and looking out front through the "window"*) It's the
oldest part of the village. They say there used to be a little cobbled
square here with cottages where the men who built the church lived;
but they were burnt down centuries ago. Some of the stones were used
to build those old barns at the end of the lane.

Elizabeth (*joining her mother at the "window"*) The estate agent said
the barns must have been used as cowsheds at some time. He said the
elder trees were meant to (*gesturing*) keep the flies away. Caroline
said they were meant to keep witches away as well.

Mrs Rowe Caroline's imagination always did work overtime. It will
be nice for you to have her living nearby, though.

Elizabeth Yes, it will. She said she might look in this afternoon.

The doorbell rings

Speak of the devil!

Elizabeth exits

Mrs Rowe picks up leaves from the US *table and throws them in the fire*

(*Off, in surprise*) Oh, hello.

1st Caller (*off*) Good-afternoon. Is Miss Penhallows in?

Elizabeth (*off*) No. I'm afraid she died last November.

2nd Caller (*off*) Cheese! Just our luck! Oh, I beg your pardon. Are you a relation?

Elizabeth (*off*) No, no. I've bought the cottage. I've just moved in.

1st Caller (*off*) Do you know if she had any relations in the village?

Elizabeth (*off*) No, I'm sorry, I don't know. But come in, my mother may be able to help you.

Elizabeth enters with the 1st and 2nd Caller

Mrs Rowe Good-afternoon. I'm afraid I cannot be of much help to you. Miss Penhallows had no relatives left alive.

1st Caller Well, that's that then. We've been doing a survey of ancient buildings and monuments, you see, and about a year ago we tried to track down a Celtic cross that was believed to stand near here. We were told that the Penhallows family had lived here for ages so we came to see Miss Penhallows.

2nd Caller She was ever so old but bright as a button. She seemed all set to go on forever.

1st Caller She knew about the cross, and showed us the remains of the shaft over by the barn. She said she would look over some family papers that might help us and get in touch. But she never did.

2nd Caller Then our office ran out of money, and it wasn't followed up, so now we'll probably never know.

Mrs Rowe Why don't you try the rector? She left everything to the church, so he may have the papers you are looking for.

1st Caller Yes, that's a good idea. We met him when we came down before. We'll go there straightaway. Thank you very much.

Elizabeth I'll see you out.

2nd Caller Thank you. But with the way our luck is going I bet the papers have been destroyed by now. Bye-bye.

Mrs Rowe Goodbye.

Elizabeth and the Callers exit

Elizabeth *(off)* Goodbye.

Elizabeth enters

I wish them luck.

Mrs Rowe *(looking ceilingwards)* I wish you luck, too, with your thatched roof. It will cost you a fortune in fire insurance, to say nothing of the birds pulling it apart in the spring. Still, it sheltered Miss Penhallows and her family for three hundred years. *(She sits on a chair)* Perhaps it will serve you well too.

Elizabeth *(sitting on the pouffe)* I hope the cottage doesn't object to my being here. It must be full of the ghosts of past Penhallows.

Mrs Rowe It's more likely to be full of mice from that thatch. Daddy was just saying yesterday that you would have been better off with a nice little bungalow on the estate.

Elizabeth *(exasperated)* Oh, Mother, do stop. I know you mean to be kind, but there's a limit. It's my life and I must make my own decisions. For a whole year after Peter died I couldn't even think straight. Well, now I can and that can't be a bad thing.

Mrs Rowe I'm sorry, my dear, I didn't mean ...

The doorbell rings

Elizabeth That must be Caroline. *(She rises)*

There is a tap on the door

Caroline enters, followed by Dr Margery Johnston

Caroline Hi. Hello, Mrs Rowe, this is my friend, Dr Johnston, Margery, my next door neighbour. I hope you don't mind my bringing her in to meet you, Elizabeth?

Elizabeth No, of course not. Come and sit down. (*She shakes hands with Margery*)

Mrs Rowe How do you do.

Margery (*sitting on the couch*) How do you do. I'm sorry we haven't met before. That's one of the drawbacks of working in town — it takes so long to find one's way around the community.

Caroline sits on the couch, Elizabeth sits on the pouffe

Caroline Margery is a psychiatrist at the City Hospital. (*To Elizabeth*) She was so interested when I told her you had the feeling that you had lived here before.

Elizabeth (*laughing*) You think I am a suitable case for treatment?

Margery (*hastily*) Of course not. Let me explain. It's true that I am a psychiatrist, but I am also a hypnotherapist.

Mrs Rowe I didn't know real doctors dabbled in things like that!

Margery You'd be surprised at the things real doctors dabble in these days. But it's all perfectly ethical, I assure you. It's just a treatment to help people with a problem instead of using drugs.

Mrs Rowe But Elizabeth hasn't got a problem. Of course, since Peter was killed she gets depressed from time to time, but she is coping with that with a great deal of courage and common-sense. Anyway, she doesn't take drugs.

Elizabeth Mother, please ...

Margery Of course I wasn't suggesting that Elizabeth had a problem. I was only trying to explain what a hynotherapist does.

Elizabeth (*smiling*) Well, there's one drug we all take, tea. Shall I go and make a pot?

Caroline Super.

Margery That would be lovely.

Elizabeth exits

Mrs Rowe Caroline, what on earth have you been telling Dr Johnston about Elizabeth?

Margery Just about Elizabeth's feelings about the cottage and how their friends at school used to tease her about being psychic.

Caroline Well, she was an absolute wizard with the tarot cards and the Oiuja board always worked when she played.

Mrs Rowe Elizabeth read tarot cards and played an Ouija board! I don't believe this! We chose St Monica's because it was a church foundation and the supervision was so good.

Caroline Oh, it was, Mrs Rowe, it was. But the thing is, the better the supervision, the better girls get at dodging it. We had some terrific shindigs! I could tell you ... but, on second thoughts, I'd better not. I don't want to ruin our reputation completely.

Margery Well, when Caroline told me all this, and how Elizabeth felt she had lived here before, I wanted to meet her. You see, about two years ago, I became interested in regression ...

Mrs Rowe What on earth is that?

Margery It's a theory that, under hypnosis, people can be made to recall their previous lives, and give a very detailed description of what is happening around them.

Caroline What we should call today a sort of action replay.

Mrs Rowe As an educated woman you surely can't believe that!

Margery I don't necessarily believe it yet, Mrs Rowe. But, as an educated woman, I keep an open mind, I'm just interested in finding out more about it.

Caroline It's not a new idea, either, is it? I mean, all the Eastern religions believe in reincarnation, don't they?

The doorbell rings

Mrs Rowe Excuse me.

Mrs Rowe exits

Margery I don't think we have exactly made Mrs Rowe's day, have we?

Caroline Oh, she'll be all right, really.

Mrs Rowe (*off*) Good-afternoon, Mrs Duncan. Do come in.

Elizabeth (*off*) Hello, Mrs Duncan. I'm just making tea. Do stay for a cup.

Mrs Duncan (*off*) Well, a quick one then. I only called to give you the Church Magazine, Elizabeth.

Mrs Rowe and Mrs Duncan enter

Caroline Hello, Mrs Duncan.

Mrs Duncan Caroline. How nice to see you, my dear; and Dr Johnston, well met; and on a Saturday, too!

Mrs Rowe Oh, you know each other.

Mrs Duncan (*sitting on a chair*) Of course we do. Dr Johnston is becoming one of our regulars at morning service.

Mrs Rowe (*sitting on a chair*) Oh, you're Church of England, Dr Johnston!

Margery I'm orthodox in some things, you see. I don't belong to any of those strange sects one reads about in the Sunday newspapers!

Mrs Rowe It was Caroline talking about Eastern religions that confused me.

Mrs Duncan Caroline, what bright new ideas have you produced this week to confound us all?

Caroline Not guilty, M'Lud! I only brought Margery along to talk to Elizabeth, about reincarnation.

Mrs Duncan My dear, I'm sure you mean well, but Elizabeth has been through a great deal in this past year. This sort of talk could only end in bringing her greater grief.

Caroline Oh, it has nothing to do with Peter. I wouldn't dream of suggesting anything that might hurt her. You know that. Margery is studying regression and was just interested professionally when she heard that Elizabeth felt that she had lived here before.

Mrs Duncan Ah, yes, you are a psychiatrist, Dr Johnston. A worthwhile discipline, but I feel that the more modern and esoteric side of it is best ignored.

Margery Surely not modern, Mrs Duncan. The belief in reincarnation is one of the oldest beliefs in the world. It was, and still is, the central theme in some religions. Why, even in Christianity, to begin with.

Mrs Duncan Oh dear, that hoary old chestnut. When was that declared a heresy? About five hundred AD I think.

Caroline Five thirty-five, actually.

Mrs Rowe Good heavens, Caroline! How did you know that?

Caroline A combination of a church school education and a grandfather who dealt in antique books. And Margery is right. Even in the Bible some people believed that John the Baptist was Elias reborn.

Elizabeth enters with a tea-tray

Elizabeth Caroline, you are not still on about reincarnation? Don't listen to her, anyone. She has a vested interest in it. I remember when we were at school, if anyone teased her she would retaliate by telling them of the horrible things that would happen to them when they were reborn.

Margery It's quite an idea, isn't it? If everyone believed in reincarnation it might make people think a bit more carefully about the things they got up to in this life!

Mrs Duncan Do you really think so? My generation was brought up to believe in Hell, but it didn't stop anyone who wanted to be wicked.

Elizabeth That's one of the problems, isn't it? Nobody believes in Hell nowadays.

Caroline That's because it is so difficult to visualize, even worse than Heaven. I mean, we can picture Heaven up there because we don't know too much about space, but it's a bit difficult to visualize where Hell and the Devil might really be.

Sparks fly from the fire

Elizabeth Ouch! (*She sweeps up*) Mother and I were just saying before you came that I really must get a fire-guard.

Mrs Duncan You must. It would be a pity to spoil such a pretty room. When you get round to doing the garden you must come over and get some cuttings.

Elizabeth Thank you. I'll do that.

Mrs Duncan It's a long time since the garden was properly looked after. You couldn't expect Miss Penhallows at ninety-four to do much about it.

Elizabeth We had a couple of callers earlier this afternoon asking about the Penhallows family papers. We suggested they saw the rector about them. They are looking for an old cross that Miss Penhallows told them about.

Mrs Duncan They must be the same people who came last spring doing a survey of ancient buildings. They had got hold of story of a witch being buried at a crossroads and a cross being erected to hallow the ground. Well, we can help with the papers, perhaps. Some of them are very old indeed; account books, herbal remedies, letters — oh, masses of them, going back for three hundred years. An historian from the County Archives is coming over to look at them.

Caroline Great! Are you going to publish them?

Mrs Duncan I don't know. We must find out what they are about first. Anyway, I must go home. What a very interesting afternoon it has been.

Mrs Rowe I must be going too. I'll drop you off at the Rectory, Mrs Duncan, if you like.

Mrs Duncan Thank you.

Mrs Rowe And, Elizabeth, don't forget the fire-guard. If I were you I'd let the fire out before you go to bed. You don't need it overnight at this time of year.

Elizabeth To hear is to obey, Mother.

Mrs Rowe Goodbye, Dr Johnston, it was nice meeting you. Elizabeth must bring you to tea sometime soon.

Margery I look forward to it.

General goodbyes

Mrs Rowe and Mrs Duncan exit, followed by Elizabeth

Caroline (*collapsing*) Wow! Never mind, all's well that ends well.

Margery rises, wanders aimlessly to the "window" and finally sits on a chair

Margery I hope so.

Elizabeth enters and sits beside Caroline on the couch

I really am happy to meet you, Elizabeth. In spite of your mother's suspicions, I do want to know how you feel about the cottage.

Elizabeth (*dreamily*) I feel as if I am here for a purpose ... but I don't know what.

Margery Some of what you feel is due to your bereavement, of course, your nerve endings are raw and you are sensitive to atmosphere.

Elizabeth No, it's not that. Caroline has probably told you that we think I'm a bit psychic.

Margery You used to read the tarot cards at school ——

Elizabeth I used to say the first thing that came into my head.

Caroline And a lot of the things you said turned out to be true.

Elizabeth And some of it was pretty nasty, so I gave it up. It frightened me. It still does. Isn't it silly when I'm not a schoolgirl. I'm an adult.

Margery I am an adult too. And a highly qualified one at that. It is not ridiculous. No-one knows what the mind is, or how it works. There have been lots of experiments, but there is no proof, nothing concrete at all. Do you know anything about regression, Elizabeth?

Elizabeth A little. I saw a TV programme once, and I've read a bit about it.

Margery I would like to work with you here, Elizabeth, because of this thing you have about the cottage. It's a heaven-sent opportunity. I've regressed heaps of people, but never at the place they have had this feeling of having been here before.

Elizabeth Well, it's a thought. It might show me why I feel like this. But how do you know it would work, or be interesting even if it did?

Margery I don't. It might work; you might regress, but the other life might be a perfectly ordinary one with nothing in it that I could either prove or disprove. We can but try, if you are willing.

Elizabeth Why not?

Margery (*rising*) Then sit in your favourite chair and relax. Do you want to remember everything when you come back? You needn't if you don't want to.

Caroline Oh, do remember, Elizabeth. Then we can talk about it.

Elizabeth (*rising, indicating the chair* DL) I don't know. It will be a very strange feeling. Yes. I suppose I would like to remember. It would be awful to feel that you two knew something about me that I didn't know.

Margery Caroline, you stay over there, and whatever you hear, please don't make a sound.

Margery moves the DL *chair to face the audience and Elizabeth sits in it*

(*Pulling up a hard chair for herself*) Now, Elizabeth, just relax. Let your whole body relax, and breath slowly, slowly. In and out, in and out. (*She sits down*) Think of breathing, empty your mind of everything except breathing. Now, listen to my voice, listen to me. You are very relaxed, very peaceful. You're beginning to feel sleepy listening to my voice. You're very sleepy; your arms are heavy; your eyelids are heavy. You are fast asleep; deeper and deeper sleep. When I tell you, you will wake up. You will be wide awake and happy. Now, listen to me, Elizabeth. You are going to go back and think about the first time you saw the cottage. Can you remember the cottage? What did you think about it? (*She takes a pad and pencil from her handbag and makes notes as Elizabeth speaks*)

Elizabeth (*halting to begin with*) I saw the cottage — the cottage. It is stone. A stone cottage with a thatched roof. There is a path through the garden. Weeds, lots of weeds, and roses and — the gate needs mending. I open the door, it is dark — dark — the windows are small. They're dirty — dirty — why are they dirty? Clean them and let the sun in.

Margery What else do you think about the cottage? What else do you see?

Elizabeth If I open the door of this room, there is the kitchen, a kitchen and a dairy, and upstairs there are three bedrooms. I know there are three bedrooms. There is another door. It's cool and dark in this room. There's a smell — a scent. Scent, it's herbs. The room is full of herbs, lavender, rose-petals, geranium (*her voice drops*) rosemary, rue.

Margery Go back further, Elizabeth. Think about the herbs. How did the herbs get there? Who picked them?

Elizabeth Lavender — scent. Yes, yes, I'm picking lavender ... lavender ...

Margery Where are you now?

Elizabeth Where am I? I'm in the garden, in the garden picking lavender. In the herb garden picking lavender. In the herb garden picking lavender and lad's love and marigolds and dill and ...

Margery What is your name? Listen to my voice. What is your name?

Elizabeth I am Sarah.

Margery Do you have another name? Who are you?

Elizabeth I am William's wife. William the Potter. See, there by the river, that is the kiln. It's big, isn't it? The clay is good here and William's glazes are good. They are secret. No-one in the whole county makes glazes like that.

Margery William is clever then.

Elizabeth William is very clever. He makes good pots and sells them well.

Margery Did he make the secret glazes, Sarah?

Elizabeth The glazes? No. My grandfather taught William to make them. He said men made these glazes in another country, a long way away.

Margery Do you know which country?

Elizabeth No. I cannot remember. My grandfather said his grandfather came in a ship. The men came for tin but he came to make pots. He brought the secret glazes.

Margery Do you know his name?

Elizabeth Oh yes. His name was Jacob, like my grandfather.

Margery What year is this, Sarah?

Elizabeth It is fifteen eighty-nine. The summer of fifteen eighty-nine.

Margery And who is king? Do you know who is King of England?

Elizabeth (*laughing*) There is no king. Queen Elizabeth rules. But she is old. Old and sick, and when she dies a stranger will rule. My grandfather's grandfather was a stranger and the people did not like him, only his pottery; but when Elizabeth dies a stranger will rule all of England because Elizabeth has no children. Many lovers, but no children. I can have children. I can ...

Margery Who is the stranger who will rule when Elizabeth dies?

Elizabeth His name is James. He is king of a country in the north. Scotland it is called. When the ships come from London for the slate, they bring us news of the Court, and then the pedlars tell us all. But Jane tells me.

Margery Who is Jane?

Elizabeth Jane is the Squire Wilton's wife. She lives at the Hall, but she is my friend because I helped her when she had the baby. It wouldn't come, you see, but I gave her some herb medicine and the child was born. It lived too, and wasn't harmed at all.

Margery How old are you, Sarah?

Elizabeth I am eighteen.

Margery How did you know how to help Jane?

Elizabeth Oh, I helped my mother many times. She knew about these things. She taught me how to make the medicine.

Margery Do you have babies?

Elizabeth Oh, yes. I have two babies. Tom is two, he is with the girl indoors, and here is Mary. Isn't she pretty? She has eyes like mine, and she is so good, she never cries — well, hardly ever. I shall have lots of babies, beautiful, healthy babies to make my William happy.

Margery Are you happy?

Elizabeth Yes, yes, very happy. My William is so good to me. I have everything, everything ...

Margery What are you wearing?

Elizabeth What am I wearing? I am wearing my brown cotton smock and wimple and wooden pattens. But that is because I am working in the garden. I have many gowns in my closet. I have a blue silk one with little beads on it and scarlet shoon with silver buckles, and silk stockings that came on the boats from France. And ——

Margery Yes, I am sure you have many pretty things, but listen to me, listen to my voice. Now it is much later. Now you are forty years old. Where are you, Sarah?

Elizabeth I am in the kitchen. I am making remedies from the herbs. This one is from raspberry leaves to help women whose babies are slow in coming.

Margery Who is on the throne of England now?

Elizabeth It is James, James from Scotland.

Margery Is James a good king?

Elizabeth No, no, he is not a good king. He will not let the people worship as they want. People are going away. Some go the Low Countries and some go to the new lands across the sea. These people are called Puritans.

Margery Are you happy with your husband still?

Elizabeth Yes, very happy. William is good. He is kind and good to me; a good husband, a good father.

Margery How many children do you have?

Elizabeth We have two children left, Jenny and Richard.

Margery What became of Tom and Mary?

Elizabeth Dead. Dead of the fever, and Jacob and Matthew and Luke and little Lizzie. All dead of fever. Oh, we had a terrible year. Nearly all of the children in the village died. Bad water, they said. No family escaped. Not even up at the Hall. A terrible time ... terrible, terrible ...

Margery And up at the Hall? Is Jane Wilton still your friend?

Elizabeth Oh, yes, and more. Jenny married her son Mark. They live up there now. My Jenny is Mistress Wilton. They wed in the spring and, oh, she was pretty, pretty ...

Margery Sarah, where is Richard?

Elizabeth Richard is at the kiln. He's a fine boy, a fine, handsome boy, but he will not stay to be a good potter, not like William. He likes the sea, ships, too much ...

Margery Sarah, listen to me. It is later now, much later. You are sixty years old. Where are you, Sarah?

Elizabeth I am in the kitchen. Yes, I am in the kitchen baking bread. It is warm in the kitchen, but I must make the wood last until Richard comes home.

Margery Where is Richard?

Elizabeth He has gone to France with the ship.

Margery He is a sailor?

Elizabeth No. He is a merchant. It is his ship, but he is a merchant, like Mark.

Margery Where are Mark and Jenny?

Elizabeth Mark and Jenny and the children are in London. Nearly always in London. Far away in London, far, far away.

Margery Are you still happy with William?

Elizabeth With William? No. William is dead. Ten years since. William and Jane and the squire, dead with the fever. Always the fever. Every year it is a hot summer the fever comes.

Margery Is the kiln still there by the river?

Elizabeth The kiln is there but nobody works there now. William died and Richard was away — away — somewhere. There was no-one to make the glaze, and soon people did not buy the pots.

Margery How do you live without William? Do you have enough money?

Elizabeth Money? Yes, I have money. What good is money? The men will not sell me wood. The women will not clean my house or do my washing. But the days are long, so long.

Margery Why will they not help you?

Elizabeth I helped the people with my medicines and flea powders. I helped the women with their babies and gave them milk and eggs, but since so many babies died they will not have me. They say it is my fault and call me witch. Richard has been away so long and times are bad. The harvest was bad. It rained and rained and the corn sprouted in the stooks. They said I put a spell on it. The agent at the Hall is a bad man, a hard man, hard with the men, and Mark is always away. The women have no food and the children die of fever. I cannot make them well if they have no food and are sickly. I am afraid, afraid.

Margery Why are you afraid?

Elizabeth Yesterday, the men stoned the house and trampled the herb-beds. They said they would be back. It is dark. It is dark. I must work — work and not think about it. Soon Richard will come. Listen ...

Margery What do you hear? Sarah, what do you hear?

Elizabeth I thought it was Richard. There are noises — voices. Oh, oh, the men are coming. I can hear the footsteps. They are coming closer. Oh, the men, the door. They are coming in the door. No, no, I am not a witch! I am not! I am Sarah. Sarah, who helped your wives with their babies and cured your fever. No, no, oh, oh, no ——

Margery Sarah, what is happening?

Elizabeth They've taken me out. There's wood. A lot of wood.

They're going to burn me in the fire. Oh, God, help me, help me!

Caroline (*rising, distraught*) Margery, you've got to wake her. Stop it, please stop it. Oh, please, I can't bear it!

Elizabeth The fire is lit. They've tied me to a stake. I am not a witch! I am not! I am Sarah. Oh, the smoke. (*Coughing*) I am choking. Oh, I can't breathe. Oh, the smoke ...

Margery Elizabeth, listen to my voice. Wake up, wake up.

Elizabeth The men have gone to the cottages. The cottages are burning. All the thatch is burning. Oh, the smoke, the smoke.

Margery (*rising and bending over Elizabeth*) Elizabeth, listen to me. It's all over. You are Elizabeth. Wake up, Elizabeth. Wake up now.

Elizabeth (*her eyes slowly opening*) Caroline, why are you crying?

Caroline Oh Elizabeth, Elizabeth. Poor Sarah, oh, poor Sarah, poor Elizabeth.

Elizabeth Oh, yes, I remember. Poor Sarah. That was dreadful. Did that really happen? Did it really happen to me? Was it me?

Margery Perhaps it was you. I don't really know. It sounded quite horribly authentic. Are you all right?

Elizabeth Yes, quite all right, thank you. I feel — happy. It was quite a strange experience, though.

Margery sits on the upright chair

Caroline Do you mind talking about it, Elizabeth?

Elizabeth No, I don't mind. It was weird. I could feel what was happening. I mean, it was real. I could see the kitchen and smell the bread, and I felt terrified. But somehow I knew I was Elizabeth. (*She rises*) I heard Margery's voice, but I couldn't stop being Sarah. I didn't want to stop being Sarah at the end. I didn't want to die — not just then. I wanted to see the cottages burn down. I wanted to see those men hurt and frightened for their wives and children. I hated them.

Caroline Well, why shouldn't you? They hated you, and hurt you. They burnt you, for heaven's sake, they burnt you.

Elizabeth walks towards the fire. She turns to face the room

Elizabeth Oh, don't you see. If you read about Joan of Arc or the early martyrs, or even King Charles wanting a clean shirt for his execution, they are all so dignified and forgiving. I wasn't like that. I was dying, but I was enjoying their hurt and fear when the cottages burned. But the "now" bit of me was shocked at the way I felt — the way Sarah felt. I wanted to be noble and dignified, but I couldn't. I couldn't.

Margery Yes, that's the difference between legends and real life.

Caroline Are you sure you are all right?

Elizabeth Yes, of course, truly. I could do with a drink, though. That was a bit heavy.

Margery That's a good idea.

Elizabeth rises, but the doorbell rings

Elizabeth More visitors. Caroline, pour some wine for us.

Elizabeth exits

Caroline pours the wine and puts it on the coffee table

(*Off*) Hello, I didn't expect to see you again.

1st Caller ⎰ (*off,* ⎰ We found the cross. We got Miss Pen-
2nd Caller ⎱ *together*) ⎱ hallows' papers from the rector.

Elizabeth Do come in. This sounds exciting.

Elizabeth and the two Callers enter

These are our two callers who were asking about the old cross. They've found it, too. (*To the Callers*) Will you have some wine?

The Callers nod thanks

Do tell.

The Callers sit on the couch. Elizabeth sits on the pouffe

1st Caller Well, after we left here we took a short cut behind those old barns to go to the Rectory, and I saw this granite post propping up the end wall of the barn.

2nd Caller There was something about it—it was so big and it tapered towards the end.

1st Caller We knocked down the blackberries and nettles with a piece of wood, and there was the head of the cross half-buried in the soil.

2nd Caller So we found the farmer. He said that it had propped up that wall for as long as he could remember. He didn't even know it was a cross, would you believe!

1st Caller He's got planning permission for the barn, anyway, so we can get the cross put back in place whenever we want.

Caroline Terrific!

Elizabeth What a wonderful story.

1st Caller That's not all, though. We went on to the Rectory. The rector does have all Miss Penhallows' papers. Not only that, but she had been working on them before she died, because there were notes about the cross pinned together.

2nd Caller The cross was erected by the local squire, Sir Mark Wilton. He was a merchant banker, and very rich. Apparently, an old woman was burned as a witch on that spot, and the cross was put there to hallow the ground.

The three listeners look stunned

1st Caller It must have been a goodbye gift to the village because Sir Mark sold the Hall shortly afterwards and went to London.

Margery All the loose ends neatly tied up. It's unbelievable.

Caroline Magic.

Elizabeth (*weakly*) Will you have some more wine?

1st Caller (*rising*) No thank you. We must get back to the office.

2nd Caller (*rising*) Goodbye, and thank you.

Elizabeth and the Callers exit

Margery Well, Caroline, as you would say, we've hit the jackpot!

Caroline I wonder what happened to Richard?

Margery Obviously, the information they have is from only a few of the papers. I expect the rector would let us research the whole story.

Elizabeth enters

Elizabeth (*flopping on to a chair*) My goodness, what a day!

Margery It certainly has been quite an experience. We'll go now. You must be exhausted. But may we talk again?

Elizabeth Yes, very soon, please. You're right though, I am tired, and I want to think about it all quietly.

Caroline Come on, Margery, we'll see ourselves out. Goodbye, Elizabeth.

Margery Goodbye, see you soon.

Margery and Caroline exit

Elizabeth sits with her hands to her face for a moment, then rises and puts the dirty glasses on the tray

Elizabeth exits

The Lights fade to a partial Black-out

Elizabeth enters

When the Lights come up, Elizabeth is asleep on the couch. There is a wine glass and bottle on the coffee table. Sparks fly from the fire and then smoke rises. The telephone rings and rings as ——

—— the CURTAIN *very slowly falls*

FURNITURE AND PROPERTY LIST

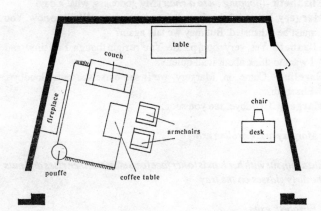

On stage: Table/dresser. *On it*: leaves, flower, almost-completed flower arrangement, tray with four glasses and bottle of wine

Desk. *On it*: telephone

Upright chair

Couch

Coffee table

Two armchairs

Pouffe

Fireplace. *In it*: log fire. *On hearth*: set of fire-irons. *On mantelpiece*: ornaments

Large rug

Off stage: Tray containing pot of tea, milk, sugar, spoons, four cups and saucers (**Elizabeth**)

Set: Glass on coffee table during partial Black-out (Page19)

Personal: **Margery**: handbag containing notepad and pencil
                Mrs Duncan: handbag

LIGHTING PLOT

Please see the Author's Note on page 24

Practical fittings required: nil
Interior. The same scene throughout

To open: General interior lighting, fire-glow effect

Cue 1 **Margery:** "Now, listen to me, Elizabeth."   (Page 11)
          Gradually dim general lighting to two-thirds and
            bring up overhead spot to half on **Elizabeth**

Cue 2 **Margery:** "...Listen to my voice."   (Page 13)
          Dim general lighting to half, bring up overhead
            spot to full on **Elizabeth**

Cue 3 **Margery:** "It is later now, much later."   (Page 14)
          Reduce overhead spot to half and bring up foot
            spot to full on **Elizabeth**

Cue 4 **Margery:** "Wake up, Elizabeth. Wake up now."   (Page16)
          Fade spots and revert to general interior lighting

Cue 5 **Elizabeth** exits   (Page 19)
          Fade to a partial black-out, leaving fire-glow

Cue 6 When ready   (Page 19)
          Bring up general interior lighting to half, increase
            fire-glow

EFFECTS PLOT

AUTHOR'S NOTE

Elizabeth's regression is in three stages, portraying three separate periods in Sarah's life and these are marked by significant lighting changes. For the regression scene two spots are centred on Elizabeth seated — one overhead centre and one down centre (foot). The individual cues for lighting changes are given on page 22.

The smoke effect brings out the climax of the play and use should be made of the red fire-glow to illuminate the smoke cloud.